"What is strong, but can be broken
with a single word?

……...Silence."

Edward Nygma, The Riddler,
"Gotham"

Also By Donald W. Grant

POETRY

Shades of Life
Echoes of Life

Silence of

Life

A Collection of Poems

by
Donald W. Grant

D2C

D2C Perspectives

ISBN 978-1-943142-33-0

Table of Contents

Introduction

In a world where we are constantly bombarded with sounds of all types, vehicles passing by, planes overhead, car alarms going off, and people constantly chattering, it is sometimes nice to just *be*. To stop and listen, to observe the things around us and appreciate the beauty of the world in which we find ourselves. Sometimes the tragedies that occur in our lives require only silence as a response, words lose all meaning. Sometimes silence is not the answer and the world demands we speak out.

The poems in this collection are a combination of appreciation for the times to be silent, the times when silence is the only answer, and the times when our silence betrays humankind. Some will hopefully make you smile, some hopefully will make you think, and some are political. Actually the political ones outnumber the rest, but then I was never one to be silent.

D.W. Grant

Endangered

Life on our planet Earth
Is where we each are given birth.
Sadly some of the life around us,
Like the tiger and hippopotamus,
Are on the list for extinction.

The snow leopard, rhino and polar bear,
Have made the list along with the jaguar.
The blue whale, some dolphins, the spider monkey
Are all included, as well as the chimpanzee.
Their futures lie uncertain.

Some gorillas, orangutans, and sea lions,
As well as the giant tortoise are dying.
The red panda is on the list too.
All of these have dwindled to just a few.
All of these are on the eve of destruction.

We humans can sit back and watch them all die.
When asked to care, we can simply say why?
But there is one thing we forget,

One thing we may come to regret.
And that is the idea of reincarnation.

If all of these die, we may be the ones to lose,
Cause in order to come back there will be less to choose.
Who we might be none can predict,
But would you want to come back as an insect?
Maybe it's time we start enacting prevention.

Silence

Words do not need to be spoken
As we sit together in silence.
Even an idea we think, can be
Stopped, with a little resistance.

The air between us can be still,
As we take in the world around us.
Sometimes to sit quietly expresses
More, as we wait in silence.

Friendship does not require us to speak.
Words can be misunderstood.
Love does not need conversation,
Just being together is good.

Discussion is fine if you want to debate.
Our lives need a little less talk.
Our lives need a little less hate.
Silence, makes for a more pleasurable walk.

View From A Stop Sign

Stop has one meaning, or so I have heard.
It's not easily misunderstood as might another
word.

Stop means stop, don't continue to go.
Not slow down, as if you didn't know.

Some people ignore me as if I'm not there.
Unless they see a cop, and then they care.
Some slow to a roll, just tapping the brakes.
A second or two being too much time to take.

Bikers are fun to watch as they pedal past.
They yell, "Stopping", but keep going fast.

"Rolling", they cry as they continue on through.
Not in single file, but illegally two by two.

So I stand to the side, watching all this go by
Hoping when you don't stop,
you don't cause someone to die.

The Stare

She sits patiently by her dish
Eyes locked on me in my chair.
No sound does she emit, she
Just fixes me with that stare.

There is some food in the bowl,
Evidently not enough for her.
She wants it refreshed, as
She continues to stare.

"Get off the couch," her eyes cry out.
"You sit there as if you don't even care.
And could you add water to my other dish."
No sound emitted, just spoken with that stare.

What Can You Say

"My father just died," you hear someone say.
"Sorry for your loss," what else can you say?

"The doctor said I have cancer, I found out today."
"That is so sad," what else can you say?

Life can be cruel, not everything is okay.
Life can be hard, what else can you say?

We all need each other as we go on our way.
A shoulder to lean on, what else can you say?

Silence may be all we really need to say,
Our presence says more than what else we may say.

Do You Love Me?

"Do you love me?"
"Of course I do!"

"You don't tell me."
"I tell you by the things I do."

Sometimes silent actions need words.

Ode To Orlando

Sounds we often hear
Aren't the sounds we actually hear.

Words can be said, although not very clear,
Making us wonder, "What did I hear?"

Songs can be sung with words that are slurred.
We try to listen to hear what we've heard.

Some sounds are actually very clear,
Like the squeal of brakes hitting us from the rear.

Some sounds confuse our ears,
We aren't really sure just what we hear.

Like a popping sound that was very near,
Was that a gun so close to my ear?

When the sounds stop and only silence we hear,
Fifty lay dead, it was a gun, now it is clear.

Silence of Omission

Bowing heads praying in silence.
A world outside caught up in violence.
Peace and love to those sitting inside.
War and hate rising out of pride.

Hymns of praise to the one crucified.
Hunger and famine spreading far and wide.

Sermons commanding, be faithful and true.
Hatred and bigotry for those not like you.
Words of comfort, compassion abound.
Wails of loss, the only other sound.

Keep your eyes on the cross and on His word.
Ignore the cries of suffering and pain you heard.

We belong to Him, we are believers.
The world is not our mess, we are not relievers.

We are one, sisters and brothers.
Wait, we forgot, He said, "Do unto others."

The Fallacy of Prayer

My mother just died, she was ninety-two.
Sorry for you loss, I'll pray for you.
What I need is help cleaning out her stuff.

My husband found out he has cancer.
I'll pray for you, God will give you an answer.
I need more than prayer, it's not enough.

My sister is being evicted, she's losing her home.
I'll pray for her, tell her she is not alone.
She needs a place to stay, to house her family.

My dog was hit by a car, he's at the vet.
I'll pray for him, God loves all pets.
The bill is high, what I need is money.

My doctor said I have a rare disease.
I"ll pray for you, God will give you release.
What I need is help getting my life in order.

My father just died, he was sixty-two.
Sorry for your loss, I'll pray for you.
I need help with his house, he was such a hoarder.

Tragedies occur, life can deal us a blow.
Prayer has its place, but can be an excuse.
Action is better, when we are so low.

Forty-Nine dead in Orlando
Eighty-three dead in Nice
I'll pray for you.
Sometimes that is all you can do.

Reunited

Forty-eight years of silence,
A niece who did not know I exist.
Siblings at odds, barriers in place.
She was unaware, so how could I be missed.
She didn't know, she is not to blame.
The sins of a mother are not her shame.

A family where love was not a word.
At least one never expressed,
One that was never heard
Only disappointment at best.
A brother and a sister in constant strife.
One actually chased the other brandishing a knife.

Parents long gone, now miles apart.
Never to set eyes on each other,
At least in this lifetime,
No longer sister, no longer brother.

The niece and I have now met,
Thanks to social media, at least on the Internet.

What Are You Thinking?

What are you thinking?
The question breaks the silence.
I need to sort out my thoughts.
She waits, delay adds to the suspense.

I wish my thoughts were more profound.
Not just random blips spinning around.

I am thinking a lot of things,
Question being, What do I share?
Why do I have to ask?
Makes me feel like you don't care.

I wish my thoughts were more profound.
Not just random blips spinning around.

I am thinking of all I have to do,
Of the things that say I love you.
Now I don't believe you,
How do I now that is true?

I wish my thoughts were more profound.
Not just random blips spinning around.

Now looking at each other,
Staring eye to eye.
I know I should share more,
I did not mean to make you cry.

I promise to share what is on my mind,
Even when a thought I cannot find.

Friends?

Some people love to talk,
Some people love to just listen.

We all have friends who talk,
But how many of them just listen?

We all have the need to be heard,
But will they let us get in a word?

We start to share our own story,
They inject one of their own,
Stealing our glory.

As we speak we see their lips tremble,
Hardly able to wait for us to pause,
So they can once again just ramble.

We all have the need to be heard,
But will they let us get in a word?

Some of us are extroverts

Some of us are introverts
But would it really hurt.
To just listen.

Maybe there would be less hate,
If we each learned to debate,
But to learn to debate,
We need to learn to listen.

We all have the need to be heard,
But will they let us get in a word?

A true friend will listen when we speak,
Not interrupt or condemn.

A true friend knows when they speak,
We will listen to them.

Is Democracy Leaving the USA

America is at a fork in the road,
Do we take the left or the right?

Democracy held in the balance,
Do we choose darkness or light?

The question will be answered, yea or nay.
Is Democracy leaving the USA?

One path promotes love,
One promotes hate.

Do we give up all the things
That has made America great?

The question will be answered, yea or nay.
Is Democracy leaving the USA?

Freedom of religion
A major cornerstone.

To believe as we choose,
About to be overthrown.

The question will be answered, yea or nay.
Is Democracy leaving the USA?

The Statue of Liberty, cries out,
"Come one, come all."

Do we tear her down,
So we can build a wall?

The question will be answered, yea or nay.
Is Democracy leaving the USA?

Many have been sacrificed
To keep our freedoms intact.

Do we honor them, or go
With whom our vets are attacked?

The question will be answered, yea or nay.
Is Democracy leaving the USA?

Time will tell the kind of nation
We will become.

A nation building up all
Or maybe just some.

The question will be answered, yea or nay.
Is Democracy leaving the USA?

The choice is ours, so, What do you say?
Is Democracy leaving the USA?

Just Under the Surface

Lying dormant still,
Hatred, racism, prejudice,
About to erupt.

Not A Time For Silence

I didn't know,
I had too much to drink.
My mind was asleep
How was I to think.

When I awoke,
They said I had been raped.
Lying naked in this bed with
Only a sheet across me draped.

He claimed I had said yes.
Gave him permission to get
Under my dress.
My mind was a blur, what
Happened, I could only guess.

I took him to court,
The court set him free.
The blame, they said,
Was all on me.

My clothes were seductive,
My reputation in question.
He had only responded,
To my drunken suggestion.

Should I have a stayed quiet,
Not breathing a word.
My friends said I should have,
My story left unheard.

My silence would have said,
I had given consent.
To ruin his life
Was not my intent.

My body and soul
Will never be the same.
To remain silent would be
To, alone, live with the shame.

Ode To The Twenty-Two

They fought in a war,
Yet they managed to come home.
They since took their own lives,
Dying alone.

What demons they faced
Inside their own heads,
Only they knew what nightmares
Came to their beds.

For those that they fought
Never gave them a thought,
Not thinking their freedom
With blood had been bought.

The number is only an average
Of the ones that we've lost.
To live a normal life
Was too great of a cost.

They had been changed
On the inside where we can't see.
Unable to relate, to
Just let things be.

So by their own hand
Their lives were sadly taken.
Our nation was silent,
Refusing to awaken.

We continue to send
Our youth off to war.
It is sad but true,
Twenty-two will become more.

A Deafening Silence

They lay on top of the water,
Not a care in the world.
Lazily drifting along,
If asleep, holding hands with each other.

We watch as they drift, unmolested.
Only the sounds of the waves
Breaking the silence,
Wishing we could be so rested.

Out of the calm, a shot,
The silence is broken.
The small creature spins,
On the surface it is not.

The tide brings it to shore.
It lies still, its life taken,
By the cruelty of man,
Holding hands no more.

A Quieter Time?

Back in the day, did people
Have as much to say?

Put up a post, express a thought.
Some will agree, some will not.

Some people will love it,
Some will hate it.
Some will be nice, some will be vile.
Some will make you cry, some make you smile.

Your skin needs to be thick,
As they pick, pick, pick.
Comments will come at an amazing pace,
Saying words they would never say
To your face.

Back in the day, did people
Have as much to say?
Surely they did, they just didn't
Have a way.

Never Forget

We say we will never forget
The day so many lives were lost.
The day two buildings fell,
Brought down quickly by two jets.

Our lives were forever changed,
Our mindsets forever altered.
How we go from place to place,
The process forever rearranged.

Images burned into our brain.
Yet we soon forget, we soon
Go on, living day to day.
Acting as though all is the same.

Only those who suffered loss
Or those who rushed to help,
Or those who simply survived.
Remember the true cost.

As the anniversary drew near
It was Simon's *Sound of Silence*
That reminded us of all we lost.
It was his words that made us hear.

So we renewed our promise,
A promise to never forget.
A promise we will not keep.
Sadly, the truth is just this.

We will forget.

Who?

The who, what, when, where, why,
And let us not forget how.
The questions that should be answered,
At least back then, not now.

Instead, today they try to entertain,
Forgetting facts, going for ratings.
The truth gets swept aside,
The concern more for who is dating.

Hard questions never asked,
Digging deep, a thing of the past.
So all we get is the fluff,
And fluff will never last.

Where did the reporters go?
The ones that kept us in the know.
Sadly, only one reveals the truth.
Comedy news called The Daily Show.

No One To Scream At!

Your problem is huge and has
You up against the wall.
Your problem needs a solution,
So who are you going to call?

The problem is more than that
The problem is there is no one
To scream at!

The lines are long at the store.
They say they don't have enough help.
So why don't they just hire more?
You threaten to post on Yelp.
They don't care if you just go out the door.

The problem is more than that
The problem is there is no one
To scream at!

The site you are on goes down
Just as you hit charge my account.

Did the charge go through?
Did it record the right amount?
Unsure, when it's up you try again.
When you get through you find
You paid twice the amount.

The problem is more than that
The problem is there is no one
To scream at!

No sense yelling at the clerk
She is just an employee,
And you come off as a jerk.
Go to their website, fill out a survey.
They say they want your feedback,
They will respond right away.

A double charge should be easy to erase.
Just a quick email sent,
As good as face to face.
Our accountant will get in touch,
Give us time to remedy this.
We will get right back, we promise.

The store says the manager is aware.
We want you to know we care.
So why when I go back
The lines are still there?

Your refund is on the way,
As a courtesy you don't have to double pay.
A *courtesy*, you say, when it was
Your fault, by the way!

The problem is more than that
The problem is there is no one
To scream at!

No One Ever Tells You

Looking back do you have regrets?
The question was asked to those
Soon to breath their last.

The regrets were not for
Things they had done,
But for those they had not,
Some serious, some just fun.

Passions had not been pursued,
Dreams had gone unfulfilled.
No one had ever told them,
Follow your heart, your own will.

Instead, they had said,
Get a job, go to school,
Life is serious, work hard,
Otherwise you end up a fool.

So the painter didn't paint,
The writer never wrote,

The sculptor's clay never molded,
The song never left the singer's throat.

The lesson here is clear,
Life is short, time moves fast.
Follow your passion, your dream.
Follow your heart while it lasts.

No one ever tells you these things,
But the beauty of all this,
Is it is never too late to start,
It is only late once we meet death's kiss.

I Am Waiting

I am waiting.
I am not in a hurry,
I can take my time.

I wait in silence.
I don't want to reveal myself.
I will, at the right time.

You cannot see me,
You don't know I'm here.
But you will in time.

When you discover me
It will be too late, your
Fate has been sealed by time.

By now you may have guessed the answer.
My name is simply just cancer.
Your life will be mine, in due time.

Heroes

Einstein
Is a hero of mine.
Mickey Mouse
Is one too.

Einstein?
You might ask.
Mickey Mouse?
What heroic deed did he do?

Einstein,
Reminds me to question everything.
Mickey Mouse,
So I don't take life too seriously.

Einstein,
To make me think.
Mickey Mouse
So I take things easy.

Heroes are not always
The strongest in a fight.
Heroes are not always
Dressed in hats that are white.

Hero is a word, misused,
Overused, often abused.
Calling one a hero
Sometimes just isn't right.

So with Alfred and Mickey,
I will stick with this pair.
With a smile on my face,
As I ponder $E=MC^2$

The Pause

A question is asked,
Only silence is heard.
The question repeated,
Still unanswered, not a word.

A comment is made.
No response, did they not hear?
The comment repeated,
Did it fall short of their ear?

I'm sorry, repeat the question.
I'm sorry, what did you say?
After a pause, they look up.
Please put that smart phone away.

I hate to be the one to mention,
But you are not paying attention.
That screen has your focus,
So my words are just repetition.

The cell phone pause
Is way too common today.
If it continues to get worse
Will it break down society?

Strangers

They live close but who
They are, I do not know.

They come and they go,
Rarely, do their faces show.

If we do happen to meet
It is with just a wave, maybe
With just a smile, we greet.

Strangers to each other
Until a noise came loudly
Out in the street.

Two vehicles collide,
Air bag deployed.
All of us run outside.

Neighbors greet neighbors,
Together, checking everyone okay.
Observing, standing side by side.

Police, ambulance, firefighters,
On the scene.
Soon the drama is over,
We all return to our homes,
All become strangers once again.

A Quiet Sport

Football gets rowdy,
Crowds can be crazy,
Mostly on Sunday.

Hockey is violent
Crowds are vehement,
Players to the hospital
Are often sent.

Baseball is calmer,
At least before
The crack of the bat.
Then the crowds roar,
On a seat no one sat.

Golf is quietest of all,
Crowds are respectful
Even as the club connects
To the ball.

When a player lines up a putt
It is so quiet you could hear a pin drop.
The air goes completely still,
All breathing comes to a stop.

As the ball rolls in the hole,
And you hear that lovely tap,
The crowds always react,
Politely with a clap.

What's The Matter?

What's the matter
With you and me?

Is something happening
We don't see?

Others seemingly climb
The ladder of success.

While you and me
Sit in this mess.

Will our day
Someday come?

Or is our prince
Just on the run?

Time is on our side
We just need patience.

We have the stamina
We have endurance.

You and I just
Need to trust.

Our time is near.
Success will come to us.

An Ocean of Red

The waves flow in
The waves flow out.

There is an odd smell
What is that about?

The ocean of blue
Is now a dark red.

The beach covered in foam,
Is something dead?

They say it's dead algae,
Give it time it will leave.

The smell is obnoxious,
Makes me want to heave.

This is normal, at least
That is what they say.

To live by the ocean, I guess
It's a small price to pay.

So our beach walks curtailed
Until, by nature, it goes away.

On The Street

Walking down the street,
It's amazing the heat I get
From the men I meet.

Not always with words they greet,
But with cat calls and whistles, like
I was a piece of meat.

Moving faster with my feet,
I try to ignore, as my heart
Skips a beat.

But I am not about to walk
On a different street.

Weeping Willow Gone

Once I stood unique and proud,
Although weeping, I gave shade,
Like a passing cloud.

No yard could boast
Having a tree like me.
That's why she loved me most.

I grew tall and strong
Until that day, when
I knew something was wrong.

She didn't come out to play,
She didn't seem to be there.
Why? No one would say.

An accident had taken her life.
She was gone, the three now two.
All that was left, a husband, a wife.

A year had passed, they said I could not stay
The memory was too painful
Someone was coming to take me away.

With saws and chains they cut me down.
My life removed, my shade
No longer covering the ground.

So now the yard is bare,
No joy can be heard.
She and I, now, both not there.

The Silent Majority

We have a voice, although
It's not often heard.
Others love to talk, although
Most of it is absurd.

Rhetoric is easy, so many
Spout it so freely.
Thoughtful discourse does
Not always flow so quickly.

The voices so many hear
Are at the extremes.
Facts often distorted, opinions
Flow like a stream.

Ironically, we got our name
From one tricky Dick.
You remember him, with
Watergate he tried to be slick.

But with our voice,
When the need arises.
We can often be
Full of surprises.

So in this or any election year,
Stay calm, don't despair.
We have the country's back,
We are the ones who truly care.

High Treason

If you are black and voted for him not her,
You are a traitor.
If you are Latino and voted for him not her,
You are a traitor.
If you are female and voted for him not her,
You are a traitor.
If you did not vote for him or for her,
You are a traitor.
If you did not vote at all,
You are a coward.
If you are a Christian and voted for him not her,
You are a hypocrite.

Black is a traitor to all who have gone before,
Who suffered to fight for civil rights, for justice,
To Rosa Parks who stood her ground.
You have sent yourself to the back of the bus.

Latino is a traitor to all their countrymen,
So easily labeled rapists, murderers, criminals.
To those who wish a wall will never be built.

You have told them, "I have mine, too bad for you, amigo."

Female is a traitor to all who have gone before,
The women that fought for your right to cast your ballot,
The women who fought for your right to choose.
The women who refused to be less, refuse to give up their dignity.
You have sent yourself back to the kitchen.

The voter of neither him nor her is a traitor,
Your ballot was wasted, you really voted for him,
Your moral stance was for naught, morality lost.
Your message is silenced,

The non-voter is a coward, how dare you sit on your ass,
The nation deserves more, the founding fathers are appalled,
You gave up your right to be called an American.

Christians are hypocrites, for you have denied Christ.

He loves, you hate. You have crucified Him again.
You quote His Word, His Word quotes back,
"Jesus wept."

Treason is defined as betraying one's country,
But it is also betraying someone or something.
Sadly, if you one of the above ,
You have also betrayed yourself.

Death of A Democracy

They cherished their freedom,
Until that freedom betrayed them.
The life they had, disappeared,
Virtually before their eyes.

Who could they blame,
Whose fault had it been,
They needed a name,
Who had sold them a pack of lies?

Democracy was letting them down
Freedom now came with a cost.
Their thoughts no longer accepted,
Their own rights now marginalized.

They felt they had been silenced
Their voices no longer heard.
Political correctness had made
Their actions criminalized.

One man stepped forward
He said he had the answers,
He said the words they wanted to hear
He said follow me, our path is clear.

They rallied behind him,
He was their new leader
They rejected all others,
They wanted him, not her.

To have their own way,
To get their fair share,
Others not like them,
Had to disappear.

He taught them to hate,
To find the ones to blame.
To rid the land of the unwanted,
To bully, to kill, to maim.

The land was cleansed
Of those not the same,
Ratting out each other,
Had become simply a game.

After a time, they realized
They had given up too much.
What should have been freedom,
Was now not so much.

The country was lost,
This man too had lied,
Democracy was gone
It suddenly died.

The Opinion of Silence

Words can not express
The fear that gave us this mess
Silence may be best.

Ode To Leonard Cohen

Leonard Cohen died today,
The world lost a great poet,
His voice no longer to be heard.
A sad, sad thing to have to say.

He left so much unfinished,
Songs never to be sung,
Poems never to be read,
The light of the world has diminished.

Yet his work lives on,
His books, his songs,
His heart he shared,
To us all, they belong.

His gravelly voice has been stilled
His smile is gone,
His thoughts drawn to a close,
His will now suddenly fulfilled.

His last was for his fans,
He told us, "Here is my last.
You wanted it darker, so
Goodbye, from a true lady's man."

The Safety Pin

Is it better to speak
Or to remain silent?
To voice an opinion
Or be quietly meek.

Words can be offensive.
Saying what we think
Can upset some around us
Putting them on the defensive.

But when we see a wrong
Is it right to be quiet?
Silence can make us weak
When at times we need to be strong.

Sometimes we just need to listen
Listening is not weak,
They say turn the other cheek
At least if you're Christian.

No matter what you believe
If you hear or see
One doing wrong
A word can bring relief.

Now is the time for us to begin
To treat each other better
To fight against fear and hate,
So love and peace can win.

The time is now not then,
So if you agree and want to be
Known as one who will stand up
Simply wear a safety pin.

The Transition

One man leaves, another comes in.
The question is, at what cost?
Values, morals, traditions once
honored, are now lost.
The lid to Pandora's box
has been raised.
Misogyny, bigotry, ignorance,
are now things to be praised.
Facts have become lies,
Lies are now truth.
Science is now bunk.
Lies believed without proof.
To speak out, to question
brings down wrath.
Anyone who disagrees asked
to leave, to take a different path.
Debate, discussion have become
things of the past.
One hundred forty characters are
all that will last.
One man leaves who was honorable,

very few were greater.
One man comes in, a narcissist,
con artist, and a traitor.
Whether we agree, or not,
regardless of our position.
It might behoove us all
to brush up on our Russian.

Silenced

They yelled, they clapped,
They hung on every word.
Some of his promises were good,
Some completely absurd.

He promised them jobs
He would make life great again.
His message resonated, especially
With uneducated white men.

Most thought he was a joke,
Not to be taken serious.
Most felt his rants were
Just from a man, delirious.

He had insulted almost everyone,
Spreading fear and hate.
Could he be stopped or
Was it just too late?

To everyone's surprise,
To those caught off guard,
He won the race,
They hadn't worked as hard.

The irony of it all was
It didn't take very long.
Before he learned
He had been very wrong.

Most of what he promised
He could not do,
He also changed his mind on
At least one or two.

So his followers discovered
What others already knew.
A leader is limited in just
What they can do.

That is how the system works
Set up from its infancy.
No one man can control
People in a democracy.

Fidel

Fidel Castro died today.
There are many who couldn't wait
For him to go away.

For years he was a thorn in our side.
A status in which he took great pride.
Many in Miami rejoiced when they
Heard he had died.

It seems not that long ago
That we faced the missile crisis.
A threat to the U.S., greater than
The one we have now from ISIS.

The world came way too close
To having a nuclear war.
We can thank Kennedy for
Not opening that door.

Castro thought he freed Cuba by
Starting a revolution.

But he proved a dictatorship
Was not the solution.

So with Castro gone, that leaves
Putin and Kim Jong.
Maybe soon all the dictators will be gone.
Let's hope that someday, we will
All learn to get along.

A True Relationship

Words can be used for love or hate.
They can destroy your soul
Or make others feel great.

The words we choose define us
Words can be romantic or
They can be lust.

Feelings can be hurt
Feelings can be lifted
Tongues can destroy
Tongues can be gifted.

While others like to talk,
Listening to their own sound,
It is in silence, a true
Relationship can be found.

On The Eve of Destruction

Twas the night before the inauguration, and in almost every house
People were asking themselves, "Who elected this louse?"
Those who had been insured through Obamacare
Were worried it would no longer be there.
The children were terrified, their parents afraid,
Bills were piling up, there were debts to be paid.
They knew the rich would be the only ones to see,
The tax breaks that had been promised to you and to me.
Everyone began to realize the lies that had been told,
A bill of goods we all had been sold.
There was never an intention of draining the swamp,
The "make us great" had all been pomp.
The reigns were being passed from one with class
To a narcissist who is totally crass.
A misogynist, a con-man, a bore,
One who may cause a nuclear war.

The fuhrer had gathered his cabinet,
Although they hadn't been approved just yet.
There was Tillerson, Zinke and Sessions.
Chao, Puzder and Carson,
Mnuchin, Shulkin, and McMahon,
Pruitt, Mulvaney, and Haley,
And let us not forget who brings up the rear,
Trade representative, Robert Lighthizer.
So as darkness fell awaiting the dawn.
We all lay awake, not even a yawn.
The next four years were full of doubt,
A buffoon is our president, only one way out.
So prayers are lifted hoping to God to reach,
Our only hope is for Congress to impeach.
So to all on the left or the right,
Sleep well, have a good night!